50¢

me
myself
& I AM

The *A Unique Question & Answer Book*
Story
of You &
God

MULTNOMAH
BOOKS

ME, MYSELF, & I AM
PUBLISHED BY MULTNOMAH BOOKS
12265 Oracle Boulevard, Suite 200
Colorado Springs, Colorado 80921
A division of Random House Inc.

ISBN 978-1-60142-142-5

Me, Myself, & I AM was created by Matthew Peters in partnership with product developer Elisa Stanford
and the creative team at Multnomah Books. Matthew Peters is a professional writer in New York City.

Published in the United States by WaterBrook Multnomah, an imprint of The Doubleday Publishing
Group, a division of Random House Inc., New York.

MULTNOMAH and its mountain colophon are registered trademarks of Random House Inc.

Library of Congress Cataloging-in-Publication Data
Me, myself, & I am : a unique question and answer book : the story of God and you. — 1st ed.
    p. cm.
    Includes bibliographical references.
    ISBN 978-1-60142-142-5
  1. Christian life—Miscellanea. 2. Faith—Miscellanea. I. Multnomah Publishers. II. Title:
Me, myself, and I am.
    BV4513.M38 2008
    248.4—dc22

                                        2008023340

Printed in the United States of America
2008—First Edition

10 9 8 7 6 5 4 3 2 1

SPECIAL SALES
Most WaterBrook Multnomah books are available in special quantity discounts when purchased in bulk
by corporations, organizations, and special-interest groups. Custom imprinting or excerpting can also be
done to fit special needs. For information, please e-mail SpecialMarkets@WaterBrookMultnomah.com
or call 1-800-603-7051.

You are holding a unique question and answer book that will help you tell the very personal story of you and God. We take the title from the well-known passage in the Old Testament in which God tells Moses his name: "'I AM WHO I AM. This is what you are to say to the Israelites: 'I AM has sent me to you'" (Exodus 3:14).

You can use *Me, Myself, & I AM* in many ways: as a map to explore your faith, as a lens to focus on your relationship with Jesus, as a fun way to let others get to know you, or as a starting point for important conversations with family and friends. What you record becomes a spiritual time capsule you can revisit months or years from now to see how you used to think and feel, who you used to be.

Be sure to answer questions not with what you feel you should say but with what you really (like it or not) think. After all, you're writing down the story of *your* life. You'll find that some questions are fun, some are serious, and some that appear to be light turn out to be the most thought provoking of all. Answer as many questions as you can, but if a question doesn't feel right for you, skip it and move on. If you run out of space for an answer, you might want to use the blank pages in the back of the book to continue writing.

So relax, take your time, and enjoy the experience of getting to know yourself and God in new and deeper ways.

—Matthew Peters and Elisa Stanford

CONTENTS

CONTENTS

REAL ME RIGHT NOW

My name: _____ Today's date: _____

The city I live in: _____

The city I consider to be home: _____

My occupation: _____

My health: _____

When and where I am writing this: _____

The weather is: _____

Sounds I hear right now: _____

The one thing I'm most thankful for right now: _____

_____

The one thing I'm most concerned about right now: _____

_____

I picked up *Me, Myself, & I AM* because: _____

_____

My biggest hope is that when I'm done I'll: _____

_____

Is wearing: _____

Drives a: _____

Has a secret: _____

Shares a residence with: _____

Is currently reading: _____

Tends to watch TV shows like: _____

Usually goes to bed at: _____

Usually gets up at: _____

Gets most annoyed at: _____

Gets happiest when: _____

Talks the most to: _____

Is never without: _____

Likes to listen to: _____

Prefers to eat: _____

Dreams about: _____

Complains about: _____

Could easily be captured by: _____

Has great potential to: _____

Is most dangerous when: _____

A DAY IN MY LIFE

My perfect day would look like this…

Morning: _____

_____

_____

Midday: _____

_____

_____

Afternoon: _____

_____

_____

Evening: _____

_____

_____

Night: _____

_____

_____

A DAY IN MY LIFE

Today my top three priorities are:

1. _____

2. _____

3. _____

Three words or phrases that describe me:

1. _____

2. _____

3. _____

Three words or phrases others would use to describe me:

1. _____

2. _____

3. _____

I like myself most when: _____

_____

_____

I like myself least when:

_____

_____

_____

_____

A new invention allows me to change one thing about myself. I decide to change:

_____

_____

_____

_____

That change would make the following difference in my life:

_____

_____

_____

_____

A DAY IN MY LIFE

One place I go to find peace: _____

One activity that makes me happy: _____

One circumstance or person that consistently makes me so angry I might explode:

_____

One train of thought that brings me serenity in the midst of stress:

_____

_____

_____

Challenges I am currently experiencing that I have some control over:

_____

_____

_____

Challenges I am currently experiencing that I cannot control:

_____

_____

_____

SOUNDTRACKS

If my life today were a movie, these song lyrics would be in the soundtrack:

[ ] "Have I told you lately that I love you?"

[ ] "I need thee every hour."

[ ] "There's bubblegum in the baby's hair."

[ ] "It is well with my soul."

[ ] "On the road again…"

[ ] "Another day older and deeper in debt…"

[ ] "I feel good!"

[ ] "If I could turn back time…"

[ ] "I'm raining on the inside."

[ ] "Loneliness is a place that I know well."

[ ] "Joy to the world!"

[ ] "Nobody knows the trouble I've seen."

[ ] "Sunrise, sunset…"

[ ] "Praise God from whom all blessings flow."

[ ] "Send in the clowns."

[ ] "Take a sad song and make it better."

[ ] "Thank you, Jesus."

[ ] "Working nine to five, what a way to make a living!"

[ ] "I wanna hold your hand."

[ ] "Whatever will be, will be."

[ ] "Surely the presence of the Lord is in this place."

[ ] Other: _____

FEARFUL

My biggest fear about my family today: _____

_____

_____

My biggest fear about the world today: _____

_____

_____

My biggest fear about my spiritual life today: _____

_____

_____

A fear I have that others might think is silly: _____

_____

_____

On a scale of 1 to 10, with 10 being a lot, fear influences my life: _____

THANKFUL

I'm most thankful today for: _____

_____

_____

Something I'm thankful for that others might think is silly: _____

_____

_____

When I count my blessings, I tend to forget: _____

_____

_____

When I count my blessings, I always include: _____

_____

_____

On a scale of 1 to 10, with 10 being a lot, gratitude influences my life: _____

I will look on the bright side.   *yes / no / maybe*

I will be annoyed by people who look on the bright side.   *yes / no / maybe*

I will read my horoscope.   *yes / no / maybe*

I will read my Bible.   *yes / no / maybe*

I will hate someone.   *yes / no / maybe*

I will not Google anything.   *yes / no / maybe*

I will sacrifice something.   *yes / no / maybe*

My opinion of myself will be based on what others think of me.   *yes / no / maybe*

My opinion of myself will be based on how I look.   *yes / no / maybe*

My opinion of others will be based on what they believe.   *yes / no / maybe*

I will live in gratitude.   *yes / no / maybe*

I will swear.   *yes / no / maybe*

I will betray someone I love.   *yes / no / maybe*

At least once I will live as though God cannot see me.   *yes / no / maybe*

I will say no more often than I say yes.   *yes / no / maybe*

I will live with regret.   *yes / no / maybe*

I will talk about Jesus or God with someone else.   *yes / no / maybe*

MY CHILDHOOD

My date of birth: _____

Place: _____

My parents: _____

My siblings: _____

My nickname(s) growing up: _____

My earliest memory: _____

_____

_____

The color that describes my most common mood as a child, and why:

_____

_____

Three values I learned growing up:

1. _____

2. _____

3. _____

When I think of my father, these words come to mind:

_____

_____

_____

_____

_____

This is how my father has influenced my relationship with God:

_____

_____

_____

_____

_____

_____

MY CHILDHOOD

When I think of my mother, these words come to mind:

_____

_____

_____

_____

This is how my mother has influenced my relationship with God:

_____

_____

_____

_____

_____

_____

MY CHILDHOOD

The worst thing about my childhood: _____

_____

_____

_____

The best thing about my childhood: _____

_____

_____

_____

The member of my extended family who would make the best…

military chaplain: _____

megachurch pastor: _____

monk or nun: _____

Sunday school teacher: _____

youth group intern: _____

martyr: _____

stand-up comic for Jesus: _____

televangelist: _____

A spontaneous drawing of me as a child (no artistic ability required) or a pasted-in childhood photo:

Me, age _____

MY CHILDHOOD

My first friend: _____

My best friend: _____

My meanest friend: _____

My best birthday: _____

My first day at school: _____

My favorite teacher: _____

The first time I got in serious trouble: _____

My most embarrassing moment: _____

My worst nightmare: _____

My favorite food: _____

My first love: _____

My favorite Christmas present: _____

MY TEEN YEARS

My first kiss: _____

My first date: _____

My worst date: _____

My most dangerous moment: _____

My first job: _____

My worst job: _____

My happiest day: _____

My dumbest choice: _____

My proudest accomplishment: _____

My biggest fear: _____

My deepest hope: _____

My funniest adventure: _____

The family I grew up in talked about God (check all that apply):

[ ] a lot

[ ] sometimes

[ ] rarely, if at all

[ ] mostly positively

[ ] mostly negatively

[ ] always / usually with respect

[ ] often with disrespect or profanity

[ ] often in personal or relational terms

[ ] rarely / never in personal or relational terms

Growing up, I attended church:

[ ] weekly   [ ] a lot but not weekly   [ ] hit or miss   [ ] Are you kidding?

Growing up, I attended Sunday school:

[ ] weekly   [ ] a lot but not weekly   [ ] hit or miss   [ ] Are you kidding?

Growing up, I usually attended:

[ ] prayer meetings   [ ] vacation Bible school

[ ] catechism class   [ ] confession

[ ] Bible studies   [ ] Mass

[ ] healing services   [ ] revivals

[ ] church camps   [ ] no church-related activities

The fictional character(s) that fit my image of God when I was growing up:

[ ] **The Abominable Snowman:** huge, scary, and probably nonexistent—but you never knew

[ ] **Aslan from the Chronicles of Narnia:** wise and good but untameable

[ ] **The Big Bad Wolf:** tricky, mean, and always showing up in places I thought were safe

[ ] **Fairy Godmother:** sweet, kind, and always looking out for me

[ ] **Father Time:** a distant but loving grandfather who kept the world moving

[ ] **The Great Pumpkin from** *Peanuts:* a hopeful figure I wanted to meet but who never showed up

[ ] **Gandalf from the Lord of the Rings:** kind, powerful, magical, and mysterious

[ ] **Mother Nature:** life giving and good but didn't come inside much

[ ] **The North Wind:** cold, harsh, impersonal—and bad news when he showed up

[ ] **Santa Claus:** the person who would give me what I wanted if I was good enough

[ ] **Winnie-the-Pooh:** warm and comforting, a good buddy

[ ] **The Wizard of Oz:** big and powerful until you got to know him

[ ] **Other:** _____

[ ] **None**

I picture myself as a second grader waiting for the school bus. If I could come alongside that child and tell him or her one thing about God, it would be:

_____

_____

_____

_____

_____

Someone told me those things when I was in second grade: *yes / no*

If yes, this is what the experience was like: _____

_____

_____

_____

_____

_____

There was a moment in my life when I changed from knowing about God to knowing God personally and choosing to follow him: *yes / no*

If yes, this is how I would describe that event to a good friend:

_____

_____

_____

_____

_____

_____

_____

_____

_____

_____

_____

_____

If my life *before* I became a Christian were a movie, the best title(s) to describe it would be:

[ ] *Animal House*

[ ] *As Good as It Gets*

[ ] *A Cry in the Dark*

[ ] *It's a Wonderful Life*

[ ] *Some Like It Hot*

[ ] *Unforgiven*

[ ] *Heaven Can Wait*

[ ] *Do the Right Thing*

[ ] *Only the Lonely*

[ ] *The Good, the Bad, and the Ugly*

[ ] *Rocky*

[ ] *Raging Bull*

[ ] *My Life to Live*

[ ] *The Big Sleep*

[ ] *A Series of Unfortunate Events*

[ ] Other: _____

If I envy or miss anything about the non-Christian life, it is:

_____

_____

_____

The part of the non-Christian life I am most grateful to leave behind:

_____

_____

_____

My life so far has been most like a:

[ ] war story	[ ] mystery
[ ] comic book	[ ] crime story
[ ] young-adult novel	[ ] action/suspense novel
[ ] romance novel	[ ] confession
[ ] scrapbook	[ ] epic novel
[ ] supernatural thriller	[ ] science fiction
[ ] courtroom drama	[ ] fantasy
[ ] inspirational story	[ ] soap opera
[ ] poem	[ ] family drama
[ ] literary novel	[ ] front-page news story
[ ] tragedy	[ ] blurb in a church bulletin
[ ] comedy	[ ] other: _____

I made this choice because: _____

_____

_____

_____

_____

MESSAGE IN A BOTTLE

I am walking along a beach ten years ago. I pick up a bottle with a message inside. I know that the message will tell me something surprising that God will do or allow in my life during the next decade.

I decided to: [ ] open it and read it   [ ] throw it back

My choice to read it or throw it back tells me this about my view of God:

_____

_____

_____

If I open it, I discover that this is what it says: _____

_____

_____

_____

My first reaction to what I read that day is: _____

_____

_____

_____

If I picture my spiritual life as a *journey,* I would describe my experience as:

[ ] just cresting the summit—what a view!

[ ] traveling toward a destination with no arrival in sight

[ ] running a race I know I will win

[ ] walking in a circle

[ ] strolling through a garden with my true love

[ ] dancing through a field of daisies with an occasional thistle

[ ] shooting river rapids, just trying to stay in the raft

[ ] leaping through flaming hoops

[ ] pacing back and forth

[ ] trudging through endless mud

[ ] walking over glass with bare feet

[ ] finding my way again after taking a detour

[ ] walking on a path that is becoming brighter and brighter

[ ] pushing a boulder up a steep hill

[ ] trying to outrun a storm

[ ] still waiting at the station with all my bags packed

[ ] other: _____

If I picture my spiritual life as a *battle,* I would describe my experience as:

[ ] victory won!

[ ] battle lost, but not the war

[ ] charging ahead, guns blazing

[ ] faithfully following my leader

[ ] extinguishing flaming arrows with my shield

[ ] trying desperately to find my sword

[ ] attacking giants with a slingshot

[ ] dodging missiles

[ ] worrying that I'm losing ground

[ ] wishing I hadn't volunteered for the front lines

[ ] raising the drawbridge to keep the enemy out

[ ] trying to remember the battle plan

[ ] looking for the white flag

[ ] captured by the enemy

[ ] other: _____

If I picture my spiritual life as a *garden,* I would describe my experience as:

[ ] an amazing harvest everywhere I look!

[ ] growing in God but not much fruit yet

[ ] being pruned by God (ouch!), and I trust it's for my own good

[ ] a stalk of green wheat surrounded by weeds

[ ] a promising seed tossed on rocky places (and here come the birds)

[ ] a sapling bending in a windstorm

[ ] a branch loaded with cherries but, oh, the bug damage!

[ ] a well-cared-for rosebush, but thorns are all I see

[ ] hard, dry ground desperately hoping the Gardener comes soon

[ ] a dormant oak with deep roots

[ ] being shocked to see fruit where I least expected it

[ ] fertile ground that has just been planted

[ ] other: _____

GOOD TIMES, BAD TIMES

The period of my life that felt most out of control: _____

Because: _____

_____

_____

The period of my life that seemed most like a desert experience: _____

Because: _____

_____

_____

The period of my life that seemed most like a mountaintop experience: _____

Because: _____

_____

_____

Of all these experiences, this is the one that has changed me the most and why:

_____

_____

_____

God created the world. *yes / no / not sure*

Evolution explains a lot about species diversity. *yes / no / not sure*

The Trinity—Father, Son, Holy Spirit—exists. *yes / no / not sure*

Heaven and hell exist. *yes / no / not sure*

Heaven exists but not hell. *yes / no / not sure*

Jesus as Son of God was born of a virgin and lived a sinless life. *yes / no / not sure*

God hears the prayers of everyone, not just Christians. *yes / no / not sure*

Eternal salvation comes to those who live good lives. *yes / no / not sure*

Every person is responsible to save himself or herself. *yes / no / not sure*

Believing in Jesus is the only way to receive God's salvation. *yes / no / not sure*

People receive eternal salvation through baptism. *yes / no / not sure*

People receive eternal salvation through both baptism and communion. *yes / no / not sure*

Jesus literally rose from the dead. *yes / no / not sure*

Religions other than Christianity may lead people to God. *yes / no / not sure*

Satan exists. *yes / no / not sure*

The Bible is the fully and only inspired Word of God. *yes / no / not sure*

The Bible is full of inspiration but may contain factual errors. *yes / no / not sure*

God speaks divine truth to us in many ways. *yes / no / not sure*

One day Jesus Christ will return to rule the earth. *yes / no / not sure*

Jesus Christ is coming back soon. *yes / no / not sure*

Miracles happen. *yes / no / not sure*

All human life is sacred. *yes / no / not sure*

All life on earth is sacred. *yes / no / not sure*

Some places on earth are sacred. *yes / no / not sure*

Humans are born in sin. *yes / no / not sure*

God desires that no one goes to hell. *yes / no / not sure*

No one I know will be condemned to hell. *yes / no / not sure*

Animals go to heaven. *yes / no / not sure*

Right beliefs are all I need to be right with God. *yes / no / not sure*

Faith without good works to show for it is not saving faith. *yes / no / not sure*

I will be held accountable for my life before God. *yes / no / not sure*

God invites us to pray for the dead. *yes / no / not sure*

Purgatory exists. *yes / no / not sure*

All who put their trust in Christ will be resurrected from the dead. *yes / no / not sure*

Christians are obligated to care for the earth. *yes / no / not sure*

Christians are obligated mainly to care for things of the spirit. *yes / no / not sure*

God has abandoned this world to judgment and destruction. *yes / no / not sure*

The church is the body of Christ in this world. *yes / no / not sure*

God is at work in the world. *yes / no / not sure*

MY CREED

The three beliefs from the previous two pages that I am most certain about:

1. _____

_____

2. _____

_____

3. _____

_____

This is how these beliefs have changed my life:

1. _____

_____

2. _____

_____

3. _____

_____

BELIEF SHAPERS

Of the following events, people, and experiences, these are the five things that have most significantly shaped my spiritual beliefs:

[ ] a preacher on TV or radio

[ ] nature

[ ] the Bible

[ ] message boards in front of churches

[ ] literature or art

[ ] my friends

[ ] a liturgy or religious rite

[ ] my parents

[ ] someone's prayers

[ ] blogs

[ ] travel

[ ] a teacher or mentor

[ ] my own failures

[ ] personal crisis

[ ] a tragic event or loss

[ ] my spouse or boyfriend/girlfriend

[ ] drugs

[ ] church

[ ] *The Oprah Winfrey Show*

[ ] a cult

[ ] a pastor

[ ] e-mail forwards

[ ] movies

[ ] an encounter with the divine

[ ] a national or global tragedy

[ ] other: _____

The three books (other than the Bible) that have influenced my spiritual life the most:

1. _____

2. _____

3. _____

The musician or artist who most influences my beliefs and why:

_____

_____

_____

_____

The leader or missionary who most influences my beliefs and why:

_____

_____

_____

_____

A person I've never met who has greatly influenced my beliefs and how:

_____

_____

_____

_____

Three people not in my family whose spiritual beliefs I have significantly influenced:

1. _____

How: _____

_____

_____

2. _____

How: _____

_____

_____

3. _____

How: _____

_____

_____

I have heard God's voice.   *yes / no / maybe*

I have received a vision from God.   *yes / no / maybe*

I have seen an angel.   *yes / no / maybe*

If yes, here's my description of that event:

_____

_____

_____

I have spoken in tongues.   *yes / no / maybe*

I have seen into the future or spoken a word of prophecy.   *yes / no / maybe*

Someone has seen into my future or spoken a word of prophecy for me. *yes / no / maybe*

If yes, here's my description of that event:

_____

_____

_____

I have seen someone raised from the dead. *yes / no / maybe*

If yes, here's my description of that event:

_____

_____

_____

I have had an encounter with an evil spirit. *yes / no / maybe*

If yes, here's my description of that event:

_____

_____

_____

I have witnessed a miracle. *yes / no / maybe*

If yes, here's my description of that event:

_____

_____

_____

God loves me. *yes / no / sometimes*

I love God. *yes / no / sometimes*

God exists. *yes / no / sometimes*

I exist. *yes / no / sometimes*

I can change. *yes / no / sometimes*

An afterlife exists. *yes / no / sometimes*

Jesus is God. *yes / no / sometimes*

I can love someone. *yes / no / sometimes*

I can be loved. *yes / no / sometimes*

I can forgive someone. *yes / no / sometimes*

I can be forgiven. *yes / no / sometimes*

What I believe makes any difference in real life. *yes / no / sometimes*

The universe was created in six literal days. *yes / no / sometimes*

Jesus rose from the dead. *yes / no / sometimes*

God hears my prayers. *yes / no / sometimes*

My life has meaning. *yes / no / sometimes*

I will live a long life. *yes / no / sometimes*

God will forgive me of my sins. *yes / no / sometimes*

I will ever understand grace. *yes / no / sometimes*

On a cross-country flight, I discover I'm seated next to a famous atheist. He asks me to explain to him why I am a Christian and what it feels like day to day. Here is what I say:

_____

_____

_____

_____

_____

_____

_____

_____

_____

_____

_____

GOOD NEWS

In my life today, a person who looks to me for spiritual guidance or discipling:

_____

In my life today, a person I look to for spiritual guidance or discipling:

_____

Three words or phrases that come to mind when I hear the word *evangelism:*

1. _____

2. _____

3. _____

Living a good Christian life that others can see is as important as telling them about Jesus.

always   sometimes   never   I'm not sure

The most recent time I shared my faith with someone else: _____

_____

I am on a car trip with a friend who is not a Christian. When the conversation turns to faith, my biggest fear about what my friend will say is:

_____

_____

When I think of Jesus, the first image that comes to mind is:

[ ] red-letter words in the Bible

[ ] an angel

[ ] a bearded man with children on his lap

[ ] a figure knocking at the door of the heart

[ ] a carpenter

[ ] a suffering Savior on the cross

[ ] Christ praying in the Garden of Gethsemane

[ ] a crown of thorns

[ ] a friend

[ ] a teacher and healer among the crowds

[ ] a baby in the manger

[ ] the King of kings on a throne

[ ] a portrait I saw at church

[ ] Christ ascending in the clouds

[ ] other: _____

I think of Jesus most often when:

_____

_____

_____

The word or phrase that best describes Jesus's place in my life:

_____

What surprises me the most about my relationship with Jesus right now:

_____

_____

_____

_____

I am most motivated to know Jesus better when:

_____

_____

_____

_____

If I'd been Mary or Joseph holding Jesus for the first time, I'd have been feeling:

_____

_____

If I'd been a disciple traveling with Jesus, I would have asked him:

_____

_____

If I'd been at the Last Supper, I would have said to Jesus:

_____

_____

If I'd been the first person to the tomb after Jesus rose from the dead, I would have:

_____

_____

If I'd been with Jesus after the resurrection and realized he would be returning to heaven soon, I would have:

_____

_____

MIRACLE OF MIRACLES

The miracle story that means the most to me:

[ ] Mary is mysteriously pregnant.

[ ] Water turns to wine for wedding guests at Cana.

[ ] A boy's lunch feeds thousands.

[ ] The bleeding woman touches Jesus's cloak and is healed.

[ ] Jairus's daughter comes back to life.

[ ] Peter's mother-in-law is healed.

[ ] The leper is healed and can't keep his mouth shut.

[ ] Ten lepers are healed and one comes back to say thank you.

[ ] Peter walks on water...for a while.

[ ] Jesus calms the storm.

[ ] Jesus asks the invalid, "Do you want to get well?"

[ ] The stone is rolled away and the tomb is empty.

[ ] Jesus walks through the wall to be with his disciples after his resurrection.

[ ] Jesus ascends to heaven.

[ ] Other: _____

Here's why:

_____

_____

_____

That famous atheist (see page 38) calls my cell phone the next day. He has another question. He doesn't understand how Jesus could be both human and divine, or why it matters. I tell him it matters to me today that Jesus was *human* because:

_____

_____

_____

_____

_____

_____

I tell him it matters to me today that Jesus is *divine* because:

_____

_____

_____

_____

_____

_____

The Bible is still the ultimate authority on life and conduct.   *yes / no*

The Bible isn't quite the authority it used to be.   *yes / no*

The Bible is a reliable history of creation and the Jewish people.   *yes / no*

The Bible is without error in its original languages.   *yes / no*

The Bible is the only wholly inspired Word of God.   *yes / no*

The Bible is just one of God's inspired written messages to humans.   *yes / no*

The Bible's most important messages are accessible to all believers.   *yes / no*

The Bible's most important messages are accessible only to clergy or theologians.   *yes / no*

I can recite the books of the Bible in order.   *yes / no*

I sing a song in my head to get the books of the Bible in the right order.   *yes / no*

I can recite John 3:16.   *yes / no*

I know what book comes before Ezekiel.   *yes / no*

I own more than one Bible.   *yes / no*

I have read through the whole Bible at least once.   *yes / no*

I take my Bible to church.   *yes / no*

I have a favorite Bible translation, and it is: _____   *yes / no*

I have memorized a part of the Bible.   *yes / no*

I would rank my desire to read the Bible ten years ago:

high   *moderate*   *low*   *nonexistent*

I would rank my desire to read the Bible today:

high   *moderate*   *low*   *nonexistent*

The time in my life when I read the Bible most regularly or intensely was: _____

_____

I think this was because: _____

_____

To me, the Bible is like:

[ ] a comforting blanket   [ ] a history book

[ ] a flashlight in the dark   [ ] a meal

[ ] a guilt trip   [ ] a textbook

[ ] an instruction manual   [ ] a treasure

[ ] a map   [ ] a novel

[ ] a paperweight   [ ] a mystery

[ ] a conversation with God   [ ] other: _____

[ ] a foreign language

A person would find these things in my Bible:

[ ] receipts

[ ] doodles

[ ] handwritten prayers

[ ] names of those I love

[ ] highlighting

[ ] photographs

[ ] news or other clippings

[ ] lipstick prints

[ ] phone numbers

[ ] pressed flower or leaf

[ ] dates

[ ] tear stains

[ ] dead bugs

[ ] my kids' art

[ ] handwritten vows to God

[ ] notes from last week's sermon

[ ] a love letter

[ ] a grocery list

[ ] an obituary

[ ] a crossword puzzle

[ ] crayon marks

[ ] a record of my marriage

[ ] something sports related

[ ] coffee stains

[ ] nothing—I like to keep my Bible clean.

[ ] other: _____

IN CHARACTER

I identify with the following Bible character the most: _____

I identify with that character because: _____

If I had the opportunity to invite any Bible character other than Jesus home for lunch,

I would invite: _____

I would serve: _____

_____

I hope we would talk about: _____

_____

_____

My favorite Bible character sends me e-mails as a way of passing on his or her life experience to me personally. Today the message was:

_____

_____

_____

_____

_____

HIDDEN IN MY HEART

If I were to write out three of the Bible verses I treasure the most, they would be:

1. _____

_____

_____

_____

2. _____

_____

_____

_____

3. _____

_____

_____

_____

ME, MYSELF, & MY CHURCH

My church's name: _____

My pastor's name: _____

I've been attending since _____, and the main reason I attend is: _____

_____

Actually, I don't go to church. Here's why: _____

_____

Words that apply to my current church:

[ ] big	*or*	[ ] small
[ ] mostly one race	*or*	[ ] mixed race
[ ] established	*or*	[ ] new
[ ] formal	*or*	[ ] informal
[ ] mostly one social or economic group	*or*	[ ] mixed social and economic groups
[ ] globally oriented	*or*	[ ] community oriented
[ ] warm	*or*	[ ] distant
[ ] rigid	*or*	[ ] spontaneous
[ ] politically or socially active	*or*	[ ] not politically or socially active
[ ] strong sense of God's presence	*or*	[ ] not a strong sense of God's presence
[ ] growing	*or*	[ ] stagnant
[ ] traditional	*or*	[ ] nontraditional

ME, MYSELF, & MY CHURCH

A favorite thing about my church: _____

A least favorite thing about my church: _____

A smell I associate with church: _____

The things most likely to distract my attention in church:

[ ] a crooked banner or microphone up front

[ ] announcements in the bulletin

[ ] concern about all I need to do when I get home

[ ] frustration over things I want to change in my church

[ ] the pastor's clothes

[ ] a shirt tag sticking out on the person in front of me

[ ] thoughts about work

[ ] ideas about where to go to lunch after the service

[ ] people moving around or fidgeting

[ ] an upcoming sports event

[ ] sexual temptation

[ ] feelings of jealousy or envy

[ ] wondering whether the cute guy/girl I notice is single

[ ] my grocery list

[ ] my kids

[ ] other people's kids

[ ] other: _____

The apostle Paul described the different spiritual gifts God gives believers in order for them to better serve the church. I believe I have the following spiritual gift(s):

[ ] administration   [ ] shepherding others

[ ] leadership   [ ] speaking in tongues

[ ] discernment   [ ] interpretation of tongues

[ ] mercy   [ ] knowledge

[ ] faith   [ ] teaching

[ ] miraculous powers   [ ] wisdom

[ ] healing   [ ] encouraging

[ ] prophecy   [ ] giving

[ ] service   [ ] I don't believe spiritual gifts are given today.

I would say right now my spiritual gifts are:

[ ] alive and active   [ ] put to good use now and then

[ ] emerging   [ ] dormant or unidentified

My greatest practical contribution to the church has been:

_____

_____

In the future, I would like to serve the church by:

_____

_____

I am shipwrecked on an uninhabited tropical island with a group of Christians—all friends and relatives of mine. I predict one person or couple among us will fill each of the following roles while we wait for help to arrive.

Care for those with physical pain: _____

Comfort the frightened: _____

Start developing a plan to get off the island: _____

Lead the group in song: _____

Organize the group to make best use of resources: _____

Praise God for the beauty of the surroundings: _____

Pray diligently for rescue: _____

Serve up meals of teriyaki monkey and coconut milk: _____

Start a teaching and discussion group: _____

Stand guard: _____

Watch for a plane or boat: _____

Other: _____

BEST AND WORST OF FRIENDS

The best thing a friend has ever done for me: _____

_____

_____

The worst thing I've ever done to a friend: _____

_____

_____

The best advice I've ever received from a friend: _____

_____

_____

The worst advice I've ever received from a friend: _____

_____

_____

The greatest sacrifice I've ever made for a friend: _____

_____

_____

BEST AND WORST OF FRIENDS

My three closest friends:

1. _____

2. _____

3. _____

From these friends I have learned that…

I am: _____

_____

I could be: _____

_____

God might be calling me to be: _____

_____

A close friend whose beliefs are very different than my own: _____

The best thing I have learned from that friend: _____

_____

_____

To pray for me when I ask: _____

To be willing to die in my place: _____

To make me worry: _____

To go to my cancer treatments with me: _____

To argue with me about what the Bible says: _____

To speak the truth to me in love: _____

To think the Hokey Pokey *is* what it's all about: _____

To encourage me when I'm down: _____

To know a Bible reference: _____

To end up as a guest on a late-night talk show: _____

To *not* notice a difference in me: _____

To be the one I'd feel most comfortable calling in the middle of the night: _____

To have more unusual friends than any of my other friends: _____

To be the one I'd talk to about hard, personal things: _____

To make faces at an ATM camera: _____

To get me to do something out of character: _____

THE WAY WE WERE

The friendship in my life that has changed the most over time and how it's changed:

_____

_____

_____

_____

A friend I am no longer close to:_____

What I would say to that person if I could:

_____

_____

_____

_____

How I think he or she would respond:

_____

_____

_____

_____

On first acquaintance…

I draw conclusions about a person because of his or her looks or dress.
always   *often*   *rarely*   *never*

I am suspicious of someone because of his or her race.
always   *often*   *rarely*   *never*

I think less of someone because of his or her sexual orientation.
always   *often*   *rarely*   *never*

I dislike or judge someone if he or she is very wealthy.
always   *often*   *rarely*   *never*

I dislike or judge someone if he or she is very poor.
always   *often*   *rarely*   *never*

I dislike or judge someone if he or she is obese.
always   *often*   *rarely*   *never*

I dislike or judge someone if he or she is thin.
always   *often*   *rarely*   *never*

I dislike or judge someone if he or she is of another religion.
always   *often*   *rarely*   *never*

I think less of someone if he or she is less educated than I am.
always   *often*   *rarely*   *never*

I think less of someone if he or she confesses to an addiction that I do not share.
always   *often*   *rarely*   *never*

To me, prayer is: _____

_____

Most recently, my prayer life has consisted of:

giving thanks	*a lot / a little / not at all*
asking for something for me	*a lot / a little / not at all*
asking on behalf of others	*a lot / a little / not at all*
confessing sin	*a lot / a little / not at all*
meditating	*a lot / a little / not at all*
worship and adoration	*a lot / a little / not at all*
silence	*a lot / a little / not at all*
crying out in great need	*a lot / a little / not at all*

One of the most meaningful times of prayer I have had in my life:_____

_____

The most important thing I have learned about God through prayer:_____

_____

The biggest thing I have ever prayed for: _____

_____

The answer to that prayer was: _____

_____

Praying makes me nervous.
always   *usually*   *sometimes*   *never*

Praying makes me sleepy.
always   *usually*   *sometimes*   *never*

Times of prayer are extremely meaningful to me.
always   *usually*   *sometimes*   *never*

I pray for traffic lights to turn green.
always   *usually*   *sometimes*   *never*

I get uncomfortable when someone lays hands on me to pray.
always   *usually*   *sometimes*   *never*

I pray for my team to win the game.
always   *usually*   *sometimes*   *never*

I would rather go to the dentist than pray out loud in front of others.
always   *usually*   *sometimes*   *never*

I pray for world leaders.
always   *usually*   *sometimes*   *never*

I pray for my enemies.
always   *usually*   *sometimes*   *never*

I keep a record of prayer requests and answered prayers.
always   *usually*   *sometimes*   *never*

I confess sins on behalf of others.
always   *usually*   *sometimes*   *never*

I have found myself praying for the characters in a movie.
always   *usually*   *sometimes*   *never*

I feel guilty about praying for myself.
always   *usually*   *sometimes*   *never*

I give up on prayer.
always   *usually*   *sometimes*   *never*

I pray at odd times and places.
always   *usually*   *sometimes*   *never*

I pray spontaneously throughout the day.
always   *usually*   *sometimes*   *never*

I pray a lot.
always   *usually*   *sometimes*   *never*

I look around when someone else is praying out loud.
always   *usually*   *sometimes*   *never*

I'm relieved that others don't know the true state of my prayer life.
always   *usually*   *sometimes*   *never*

I wonder if I am praying right.
always   *usually*   *sometimes*   *never*

I pray before meals at home.
always   *usually*   *sometimes*   *never*

I pray before meals in restaurants.
always   *usually*   *sometimes*   *never*

I am afraid God will not answer my prayers.
always   *usually*   *sometimes*   *never*

I am afraid God will answer my prayers.
always   *usually*   *sometimes*   *never*

WHEN GOD SPEAKS TO ME...

I usually hear or experience:

[ ] a still, small voice

[ ] words of a friend or pastor

[ ] fear and trembling

[ ] an audible voice

[ ] encouragement

[ ] confirming circumstances

[ ] unexplainable coincidences

[ ] a feeling of peace

[ ] a Bible verse

[ ] a vision

[ ] God doesn't speak to me.

God's name on my caller ID would appear as:

[ ] Abba   [ ] Lord

[ ] Christ   [ ] Mother

[ ] Restricted   [ ] Great Spirit

[ ] Father   [ ] Papa

[ ] God   [ ] Unavailable

[ ] Daddy   [ ] Unknown

[ ] Holy Spirit   [ ] Heavenly Father

[ ] Home   [ ] Heaven

[ ] Jesus   [ ] Other: _____

Three things in my life most likely to make me feel close to God:

1. _____

2. _____

3. _____

Three things in my life most likely to make me feel distant from God:

1. _____

2. _____

3. _____

When I feel distant from God:

    [ ] I tend to blame God.

    [ ] I tend to blame myself.

    [ ] I tend to doubt God is pursuing me.

    [ ] I tend to believe God is pursuing me.

If I were allowed to think about God at only one time of the day or night, I would choose

_____ because: _____

_____

_____

OOPS!

Three things I used to do that I am not proud of:

1. _____

2. _____

3. _____

Three things I do currently that I am not proud of:

1. _____

2. _____

3. _____

My most recurring sin: _____

One thing I do that I only recently realized is not right: _____

_____

I know what it's like to live under a cloud of sin and guilt, and it feels like: _____

_____

I know what it's like to experience forgiveness and grace, and it feels like: _____

_____

_____

Confession of sins and failures to God comes easily to me.

always   *usually*   *sometimes*   *never*

When I confess to God, I assume I'm not doing it right.

always   *usually*   *sometimes*   *never*

I become more aware of God's love for me when I confess.

always   *usually*   *sometimes*   *never*

I become more aware of what I did wrong when I confess.

always   *usually*   *sometimes*   *never*

I confess the same mistakes over and over.

always   *usually*   *sometimes*   *never*

I confess to a priest and receive his absolution.

always   *usually*   *sometimes*   *never*

I would rather confess to God than admit my sins to others.

always   *usually*   *sometimes*   *never*

I feel better after confessing.

always   *usually*   *sometimes*   *never*

I don't need to confess anything, because God knows my heart.

always   *usually*   *sometimes*   *never*

Forgiving myself comes fairly easily to me.

always   *usually*   *sometimes*   *never*

Forgiving others comes fairly easily to me.

always   *usually*   *sometimes*   *never*

Accepting God's forgiveness comes fairly easily to me.

always   *usually*   *sometimes*   *never*

If I could choose, it would be more important to me to…

[ ] have money	*or*	[ ] have good health
[ ] win the lottery	*or*	[ ] boycott the lottery
[ ] buy something on credit	*or*	[ ] pay cash
[ ] love my job	*or*	[ ] drive a nice car
[ ] give $1,000 anonymously	*or*	[ ] give $1,000 personally
[ ] give $1,000 to my church	*or*	[ ] invest $1,000
[ ] own a large home and host missionary families	*or*	[ ] own a small home and give money to missionaries I've never met
[ ] give a dollar a day to a homeless man	*or*	[ ] give a dollar a day to protect the environment

Money usually brings happiness.   *yes / no*

Money usually is an obstacle to happiness.   *yes / no*

Money doesn't have anything to do with happiness.   *yes / no*

Having money is a greater test of my faith than not having money.   *yes / no*

I believe that if I have enough faith I will become wealthy.   *yes / no*

A possession I consider valuable that no one else would: _____

_____

I have the opportunity to live in my current world but with no exposure to television, movies, the Internet, or magazines. I *would / wouldn't* agree to this arrangement because:

_____

_____

_____

_____

_____

I see a man hit by a car in a parking lot. While others call for help, I try to comfort him, but he appears to be dying. He asks me to pray for him. What do I pray?

_____

_____

_____

_____

_____

To guarantee the salvation of an unbelieving family member.   *yes / no*

To guarantee my children's financial well-being.   *yes / no*

To rescue a neighbor's child about to get hit by a car.   *yes / no*

To rescue a pet about to get hit by a car.   *yes / no*

To bring salvation to a community that had not heard about Christ.   *yes / no*

So that a family member wouldn't have to experience a life of pain.   *yes / no*

If in doing so I could bring peace in the Middle East.   *yes / no*

If in doing so I could set off a nationwide revival.   *yes / no*

If I could first find and eat the perfect cheesecake.   *yes / no*

If I felt that God was asking me to, even if I didn't understand why.   *yes / no*

None of the above—my life is God's to take at the time of God's choosing.   *yes / no*

Other: _____

If I were given the option to retire comfortably today, would I take it?   *yes / no*

Why or why not? _____

_____

_____

If I did retire today, this is the first thing I would do tomorrow morning:

_____

_____

_____

The most important thing I believe God wants me to do today is:

_____

_____

_____

A one-sentence statement of what I believe God wants me to do with my life:

_____

_____

To be safe.

strongly   *somewhat*   *only a little*   *not at all*

To be liked.

strongly   *somewhat*   *only a little*   *not at all*

To bring honor and glory to God.

strongly   *somewhat*   *only a little*   *not at all*

To be with God.

strongly   *somewhat*   *only a little*   *not at all*

To hear God's "Well done!" at the end of my days.

strongly   *somewhat*   *only a little*   *not at all*

To lose weight.

strongly   *somewhat*   *only a little*   *not at all*

To look more attractive.

strongly   *somewhat*   *only a little*   *not at all*

To get in better physical shape.

strongly   *somewhat*   *only a little*   *not at all*

To pursue holiness and avoid sin.

strongly   *somewhat*   *only a little*   *not at all*

To create something enduring.

strongly   *somewhat*   *only a little*   *not at all*

To be the best parent I can be.

strongly   *somewhat*   *only a little*   *not at all*

To help the weak and oppressed in Jesus's name.

strongly   *somewhat*   *only a little*   *not at all*

To provide for my family.

strongly   *somewhat*   *only a little*   *not at all*

To lead others to a saving knowledge of Jesus Christ.

strongly   *somewhat*   *only a little*   *not at all*

To disciple other Christians in their faith.

strongly   *somewhat*   *only a little*   *not at all*

To love someone deeply.

strongly   *somewhat*   *only a little*   *not at all*

To get a different job.

strongly   *somewhat*   *only a little*   *not at all*

To be loved.

strongly   *somewhat*   *only a little*   *not at all*

To be wealthy.

strongly   *somewhat*   *only a little*   *not at all*

To be respected by those whose opinions matter to me.

strongly   *somewhat*   *only a little*   *not at all*

To know God.

strongly   *somewhat*   *only a little*   *not at all*

To be famous.

strongly   *somewhat*   *only a little*   *not at all*

To be and feel forgiven.

strongly   *somewhat*   *only a little*   *not at all*

To live my life—or parts of it—over again.

strongly   *somewhat*   *only a little*   *not at all*

To make my actions consistent with my beliefs.

strongly   *somewhat*   *only a little*   *not at all*

To be happy.

strongly   *somewhat*   *only a little*   *not at all*

Other things my heart desires not mentioned in the past few pages:

To Be	To Do	To Have

I'm in my eighties, living in a retirement center. A great-grandchild comes for a visit. I ask her to read the verse for the day on my calendar. It is "Delight yourself in the LORD and he will give you the desires of your heart" (Psalm 37:4). After reading it aloud, she turns to me and asks, "Did he?" I answer:

_____

_____

_____

_____

_____

_____

_____

_____

_____

_____

_____

IF I DIED TODAY

The person/people I most want with me at the moment of passing: _____

_____

_____

The unfinished business on earth that would bother me most: _____

_____

_____

My biggest relief that life on earth is done: _____

_____

_____

My most enduring regret: _____

_____

_____

The first three people I would talk to in heaven apart from God and why:

1. _____

2. _____

3. _____

IF I DIED TODAY

Soon after I get to heaven, I write a letter to a loved one (or loved ones) on earth. Here is some of what I say:

Dear _____,

In a word, life here in heaven is _____.

While you're still on earth, be sure to _____

_____

_____

Feel free to enjoy _____

Don't worry so much about _____

Don't waste your time with _____

Life is _____

God is _____

And also remember _____

_____

_____

Signed, _____

STICKY NOTES RE: MY FUNERAL

Don't forget to: _____

Please do not: _____

Place I would like to be interred: _____

I prefer: [ ] burial   [ ] cremation   [ ] donation of organs

Three nonfamily members I hope come to my funeral or memorial service:

1. _____

2. _____

3. _____

The apostle Paul wrote that Christ followers do not grieve like those "who have no hope" (1 Thessalonians 4:13). At my funeral, I hope this means:

_____

_____

_____

_____

_____

_____

STICKY NOTES RE: MY FUNERAL

Music I would like played or sung: _____

_____

Bible passages or other readings I would like quoted: _____

_____

I would like _____ to give the eulogy.

I would like _____ to officiate.

In lieu of flowers, send contributions to: _____

_____

[ ] Actually, I want lots of flowers at my funeral.

What I would like my tombstone to say: _____

_____

Other notes or reminders:

_____

_____

_____

MY LEGACY

I hope to be remembered for what I have done with my life in each of the following areas:

Love and marriage:

1. _____

_____

2. _____

_____

3. _____

_____

Family or parenting:

1. _____

_____

2. _____

_____

3. _____

_____

MY LEGACY

Learning and education:

1. _____

_____

2. _____

_____

3. _____

_____

Work or career:

1. _____

_____

2. _____

_____

3. _____

_____

MY LEGACY

Public service:

1. _____

_____

2. _____

_____

3. _____

_____

Ministry:

1. _____

_____

2. _____

_____

3. _____

_____

Words or pictures that summarize my experience with *Me, Myself, & I AM:*

Thoughts I Had	Feelings I Had
Beliefs I Reconsidered	**Questions That Came to Mind About Myself**

I learned *a lot / a little / not much* about myself by working through this book.

I learned *a lot / a little / not much* about God by working through this book.

The question that I struggled with the most: _____

_____

_____

Why I think that was: _____

_____

_____

My most surprising discovery about myself: _____

_____

_____

My most surprising discovery about God and me: _____

_____

_____

You will seek me and find me when you
seek me with all your heart.

—God's promise in Jeremiah 29:13

NOTES

NOTES

NOTES

NOTES